ARTIST
TRANSCRIPTIONS
SAXOPHONE

The
James Carter
COLLECTION

Transcribed by Jim Carroll

Cover photo - F. Scott Schafer

ISBN 0-7935-8795-6

HAL•LEONARD®
CORPORATION

7777 W. BLUEMOUND RD. P.O. BOX 13819 MILWAUKEE, WI 53213

Visit Hal Leonard Online at
www.halleonard.com

James Carter

BIOGRAPHY

Often called "the most exciting young saxophonist to arrive on the scene in the last 25 years," James Carter strikes a remarkable balance between mainstream and free jazz. "His all-embracing musical vision and volcanic tone blow away all distinctions between swing, bop, and free jazz," writes *Down Beat*. And *Playboy* writes "Rather than honoring the classic compositions with a stiff neck, Carter blows their guts out, turning jazz back to its roots." Carter's recordings have made both *The New York Times* and *The Village Voice's* year-end-best-of-lists.

A native of Detroit, Michigan, Carter was exposed to a broad range of music early on. One of his brothers played guitar with Parliament-Funkadelic, another brother was a lead singer in a local soul band, and his mother played piano and violin. Before he turned 10, Carter had fallen in love with the sound, shape and very idea of the saxophone (he remains an obsessive collector of saxes and other instruments). Carter first studied jazz and classical music with local musician and educator Donald Washington. His first collective jazz experience was with Washington as leader. The band was called Byrd Trane Sco Now. During his summers, Carter played at the Blue Lake Arts Camp, in Muskegon County, Michigan, and when he won a scholarship to the prestigious Interlochen classical music camp 100 miles away, he attended both sessions concurrently.

Carter first came to national attention at 17 while touring with Wynton Marsalis. He later struck up a relationship with Lester Bowie, founding member of the Art Ensemble of Chicago, and performed with the trumpeter's quintet. A window of opportunity quickly opened for him, including membership in the Julius Hemphill Sextet and featured roles in works by the late saxophonist: the jazz opera *Long Tongues*, and the Bill T. Jones/Arnie Zane dance production *Uncle Tom's Cabin*. Before he turned 20, Carter recorded two albums with Hemphill and two more with Bowie's New York Organ Ensemble. Over the next few years, he appeared with the Mingus Big Band and with Marsalis Big Band at Lincoln Center, accompanied vocalist Kathleen Battle, and performed frequent recitals with the Detroit-based Creative Artists Collective, where he met bassist Jaribu Shahid, drummer Tani Tabbal, and pianist Craig Taborn.

Since showcased on the 1991 *Tough Young Tenors* album, Carter has steadily risen as an authentic personality. His debut as a leader, *JC on the Set*, was released by DIW in Japan in 1993 and by Columbia in the United States in 1994. Two 1995 albums followed: *The Real Quiet Storm* (Atlantic Records), a ballad-dominated set that rose to no. 4 on *Billboard's* Top Jazz Albums Chart, and *Jurassic Classics* (Columbia DIW), Carter's most monstrous blowing session yet. Carter can also be heard with Lester Bowie on *Funky T. Cool T.* and *The Organizer* for DIW, and with Julius Hemphill on *Five Chord Stud* and *Fat Man and the Hard Blues*.

Conversin' with the Elders, Carter's second album for Atlantic, combines his youthful fire with a storied group of musical guests including trumpeter Harry "Sweets" Edison and tenorist/clarinetist Buddy Tate, both veterans of the Count Basie Orchestra; a pair of avant-garde giants, trumpeter Lester Bowie (Art Ensemble of Chicago) and baritonist Hamiet Bluiett (World Saxophone Quartet); and altoist Larry Smith, a mainstay of the Detroit jazz scene over the last few decades.

As a leader of his quartet, Carter performs extensively throughout the United States. He tours Europe three times a year and has made appearances in Australia, Brazil and Israel. Upcoming engagements include performances in Turkey and La Martinique, as well as a tour of Japan. Carter can be seen in Robert Altman's film, *Kansas City*, released in August 1996, and can be heard on the movie soundtrack released by Verve Records in May 1996.

Carter has received numerous awards, including the first 1995 Cal Arts/Alpert Award, granted to young artists who are making a significant impact in theater, dance, visual arts, music, and film/video. In 1996, he was a first-place winner of N2K's Global Jazz Poll Award on Jazz Central radio.

SELECTED DISCOGRAPHY

TITLE	YEAR	LABEL/CAT. NO.

as a leader:

JC on the Set — 1993 — Columbia DIW 66149
  "Baby Girl Blues"
  "Blues for a Nomadic Princess"
  "JC on the Set"

Jurassic Classics — 1995 — DIW/Columbia CK 67058
  "Ask Me Now"
  "Out of Nowhere"

The Real Quiet Storm — 1995 — Atlantic Jazz 82742-2
  "Born to Be Blue"
  "Deep Throat Blues"
  "The Intimacy of My Woman's Beautiful Eyes"
  "'Round Midnight"
  "Stevedore's Serenade"

Conversin' with the Elders — 1996 — Atlantic 82908-2
  "Atitled Valse"
  "Centerpiece"
  "Parker's Mood"

In Carterian Fashion — 1998 — Atlantic 83082

soundtracks:

Kansas City — 1996 — Verve 529 554

Great Expectations — 1998 — Atlantic 83063-2

with various others:

Fat Man and the Hard Blues — 1991 — Black Saint 120115 (Julius Hemphill)

Tough Young Tenors — 1991 — Antilles 422-848767

Five Chord Stud — 1994 — Black Saint 120140 (Julius Hemphill)

Rush & Hustle — 1994 — WenHa 230 (Wendell Harrison)

Funky T. Cool T. — 1995 — DIW 853 (Lester Bowie)

The Organizer — 1995 — DIW 821 (Lester Bowie)

Dreamland — 1996 — Atlantic 82946 (Madeleine Peyroux)

Saxemble — 1996 — Qwest/Warner Bros. 9 46181 (Saxemble)

ATITLED VALSE

Tenor Sax

By JAMES CARTER

6

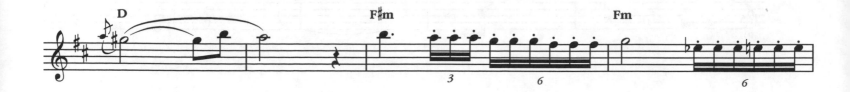

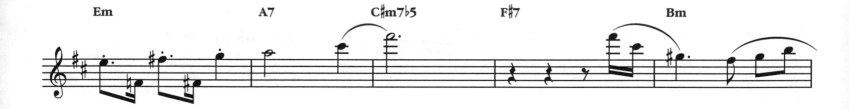

Chorus 2

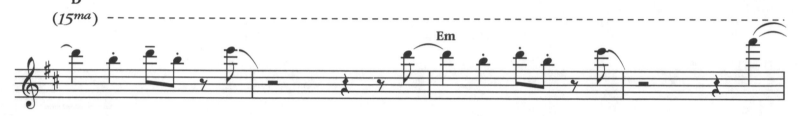

Chorus 3

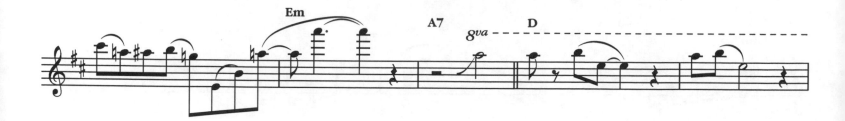

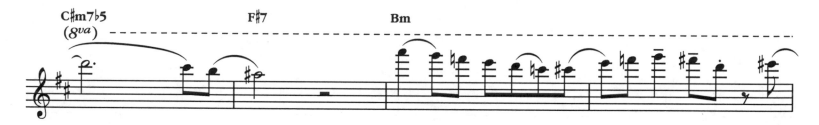

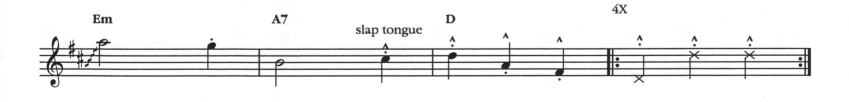

ritard.

Nitey night to you.

ASK ME NOW

Alto Sax

By THELONIOUS MONK

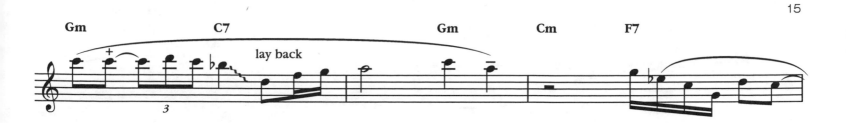

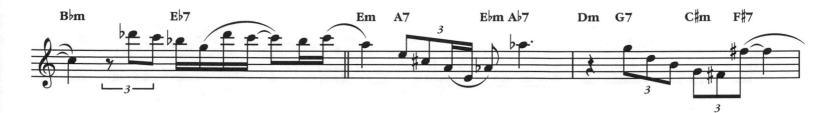

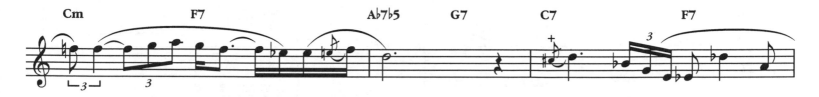

Chorus 1

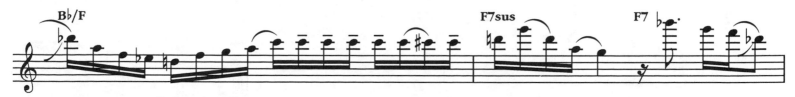

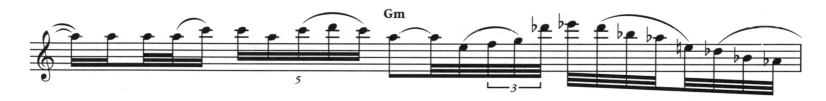

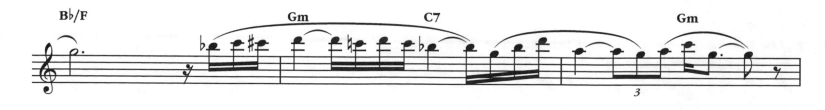

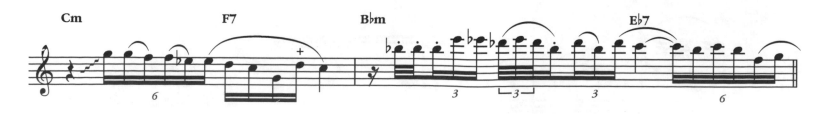

Cadenza

BABY GIRL BLUES

Alto Sax

By JAMES CARTER

Swing
♩ = 252

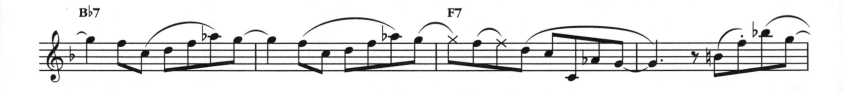

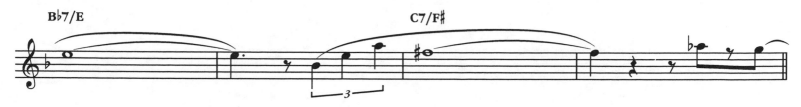

Chorus 1

Chorus 2

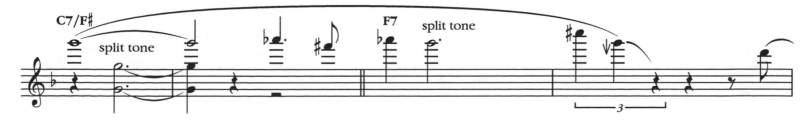

Chorus 3

Chorus 4

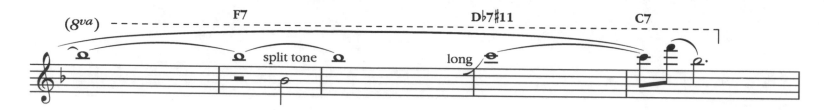

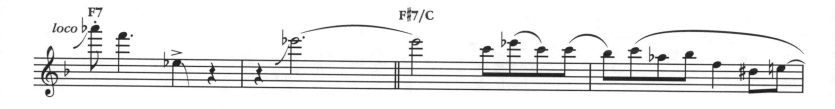

Chorus 5

BLUES FOR A NOMADIC PRINCESS

Tenor Sax

By JAMES CARTER

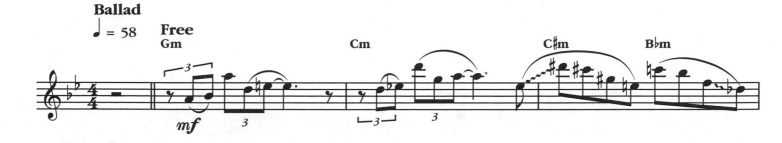

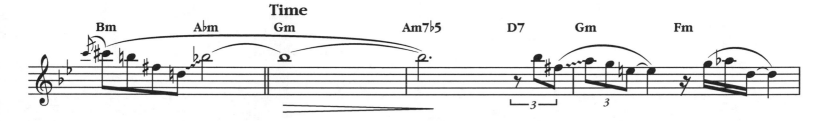

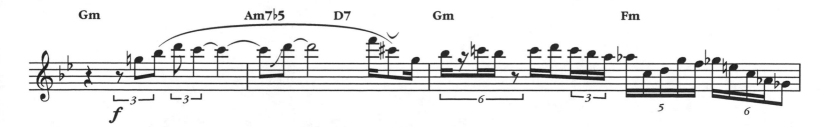

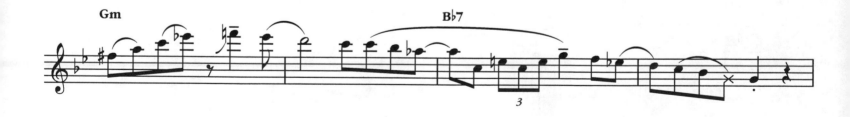

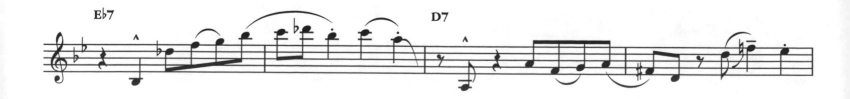

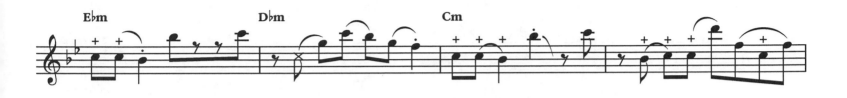

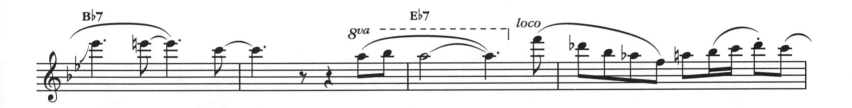

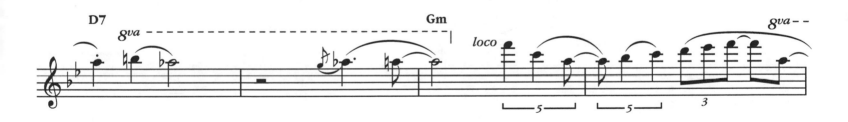

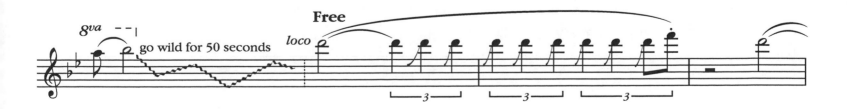

Tempo I

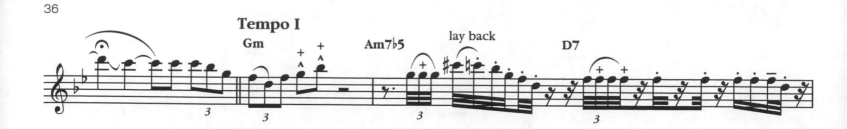

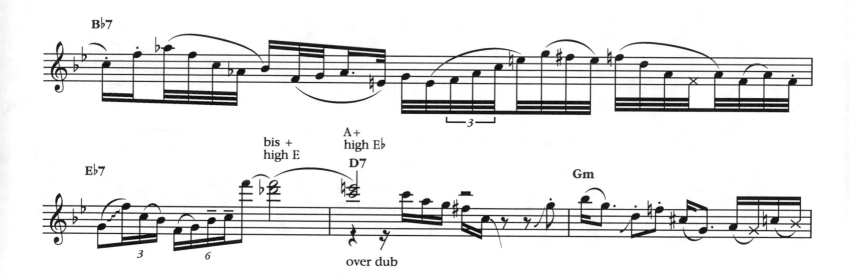

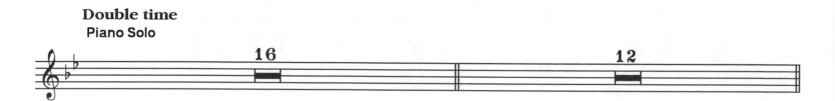

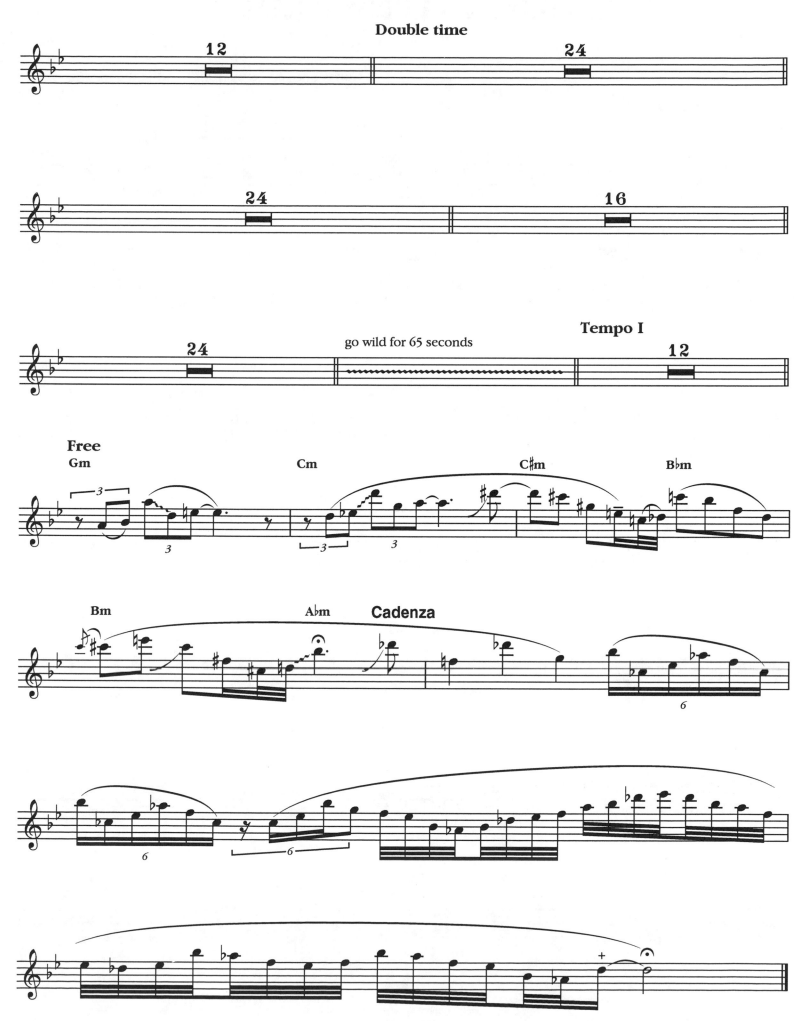

BORN TO BE BLUE

Soprano Sax

Words and Music by ROBERT WELLS and MEL TORME

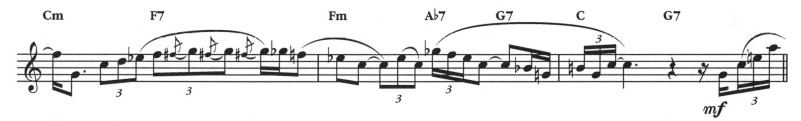

Chorus 1

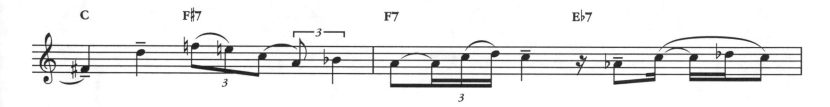

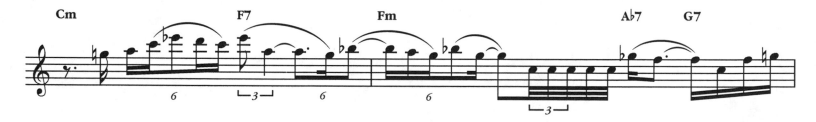

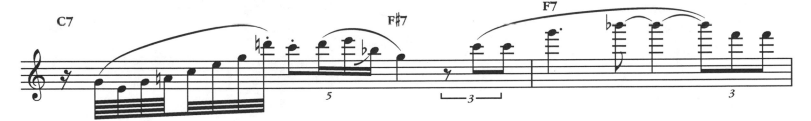

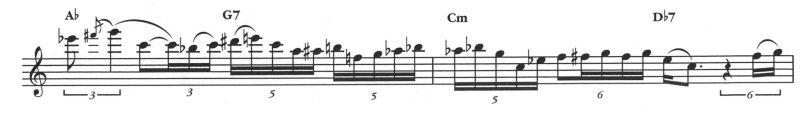

Bass Solo

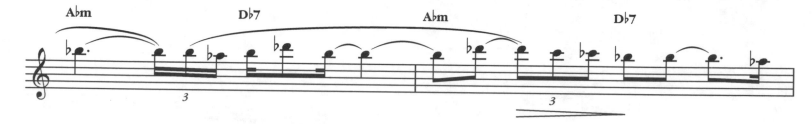

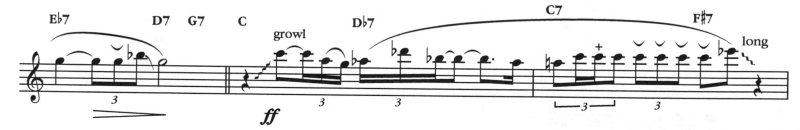

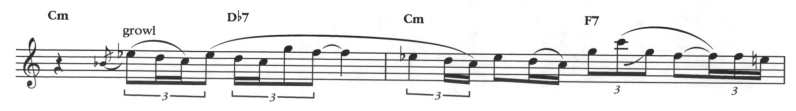

CENTERPIECE

Tenor Sax

By HARRY "SWEETS" EDISON and JOHN HANDY

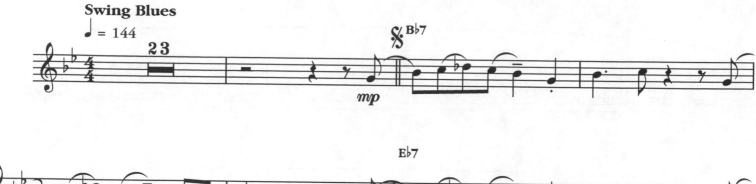

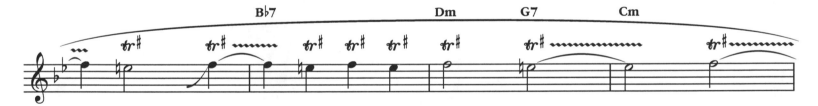

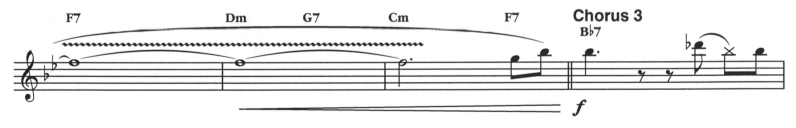

Chorus 4

Piano Solo

trade 4s with trumpet

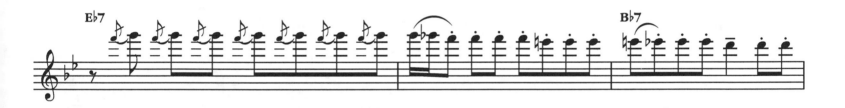

DEEP THROAT BLUES

Bass Clarinet

By JAMES CARTER

Swing

♩ = 112

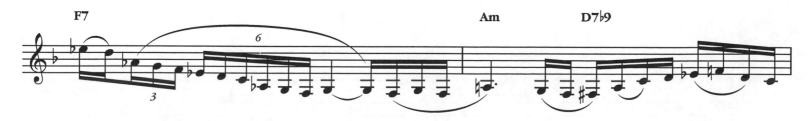

Chorus 1

Chorus 2

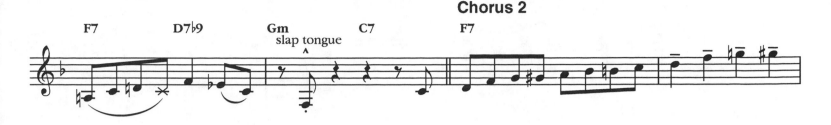

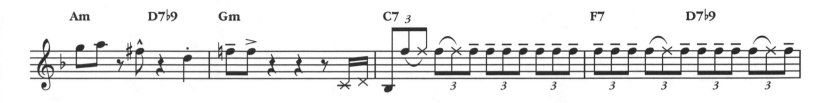

Chorus 3

Chorus 4

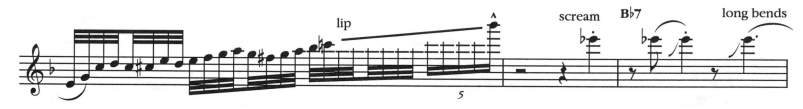

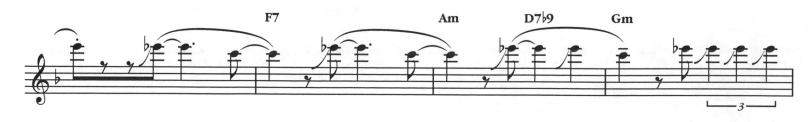

Chorus 5

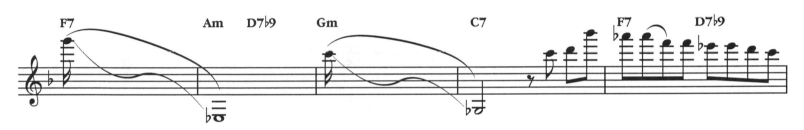

Piano Solo

Drum Solo
trade 4s

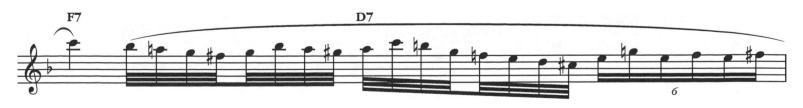

ritard.

THE INTIMACY OF MY WOMAN'S BEAUTIFUL EYES

Alto Sax

By JAMES CARTER

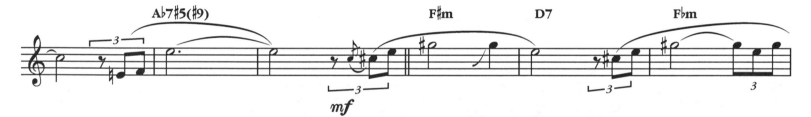

Chorus 1

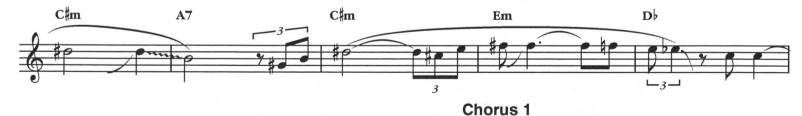

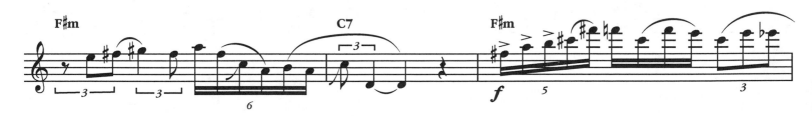

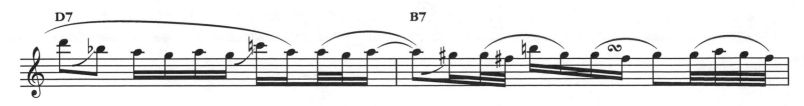

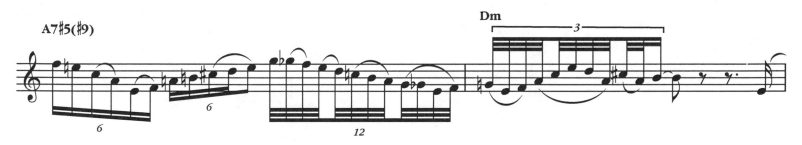

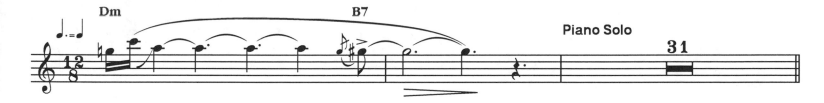

'ROUND MIDNIGHT

Bari Sax

Words by BERNIE HANIGHEN
Music by THELONIOUS MONK and COOTIE WILLIAMS

Ballad - Double-time feel

♩ = 52

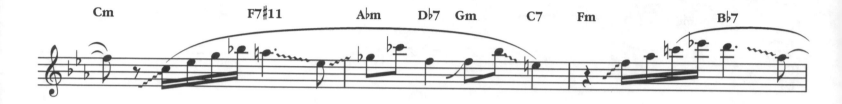

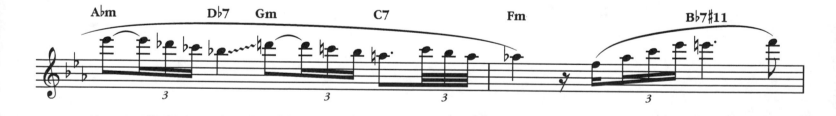

C

Cm7♭5   **F7**

G7   **Am7♭5**   **D7**

G7♯11

Fm   **B♭7**   **E♭**   **A♭7**   **G7**

C7   **B♭7**   **A♭7**

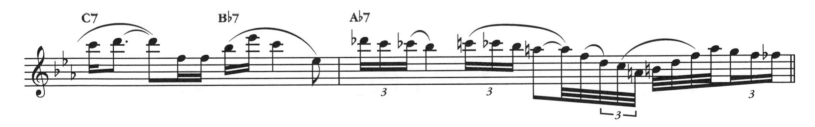

Cm   **Cm/B**   **Cm/B♭**   **Cm/A**   **A♭7♯11**   **G7**   **Cm**   **F7**

A♭m   **D♭7**   **Gm**   **C7**   **Fm**   **B♭7**

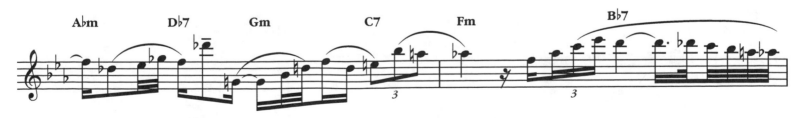

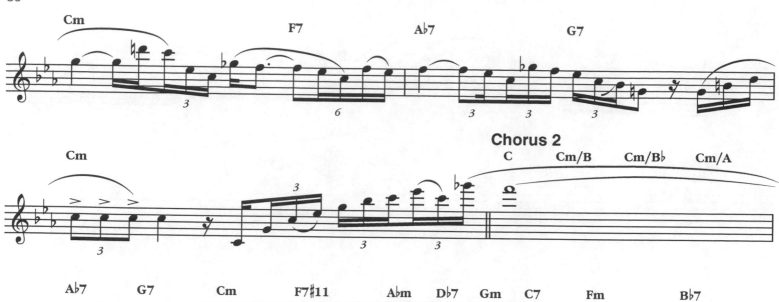

Chorus 2

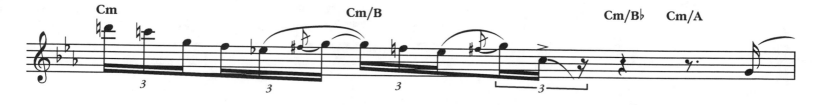

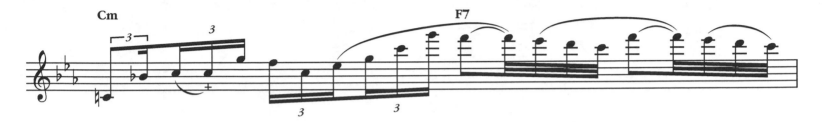

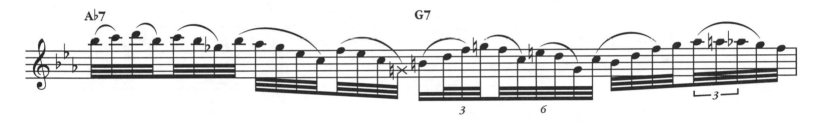

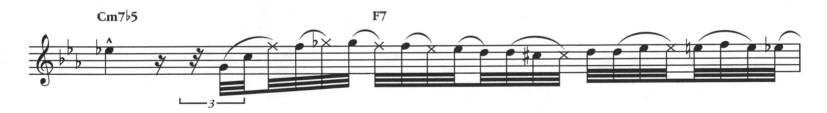

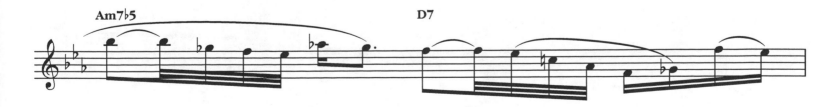

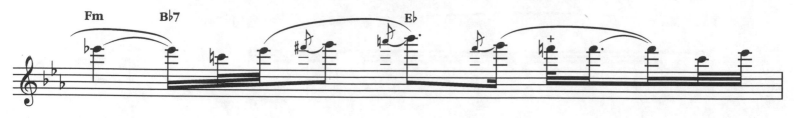

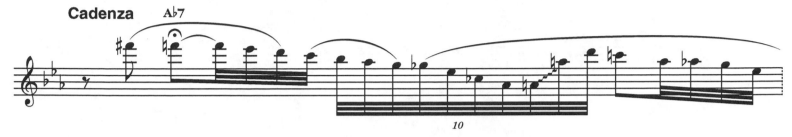

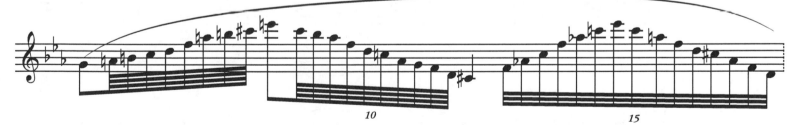

STEVEDORE'S SERENADE

Tenor Sax

Words by IRVING GORDON and BILLY EDELSTEIN
Music by DUKE ELLINGTON

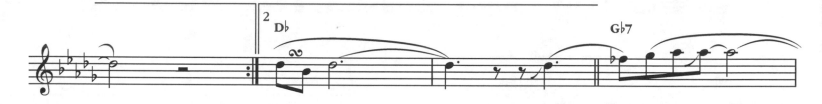

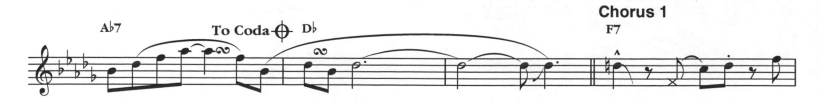

Chorus 2

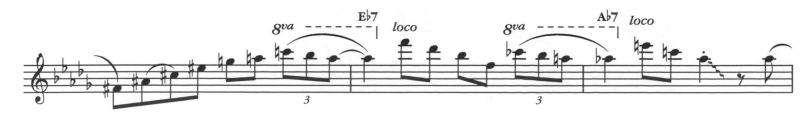

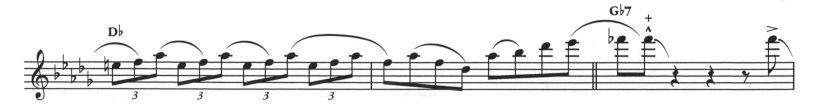

Chorus 3
Double time

Chorus 4

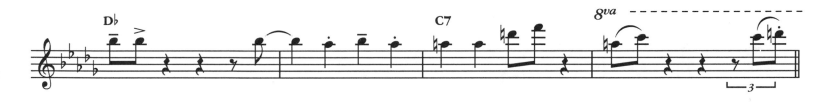

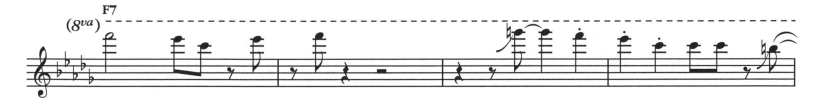

Tempo I

73

JC ON THE SET

Tenor Sax

By JAMES CARTER

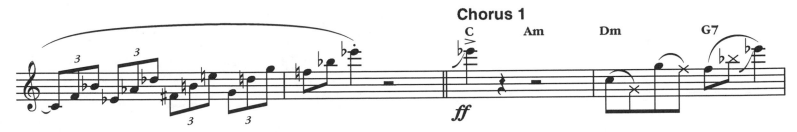

Chorus 1

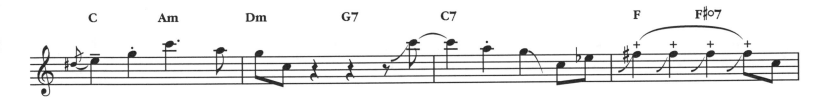

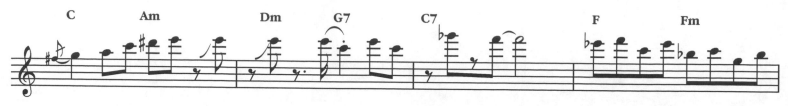

Chorus 2

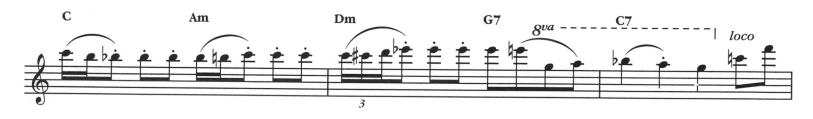

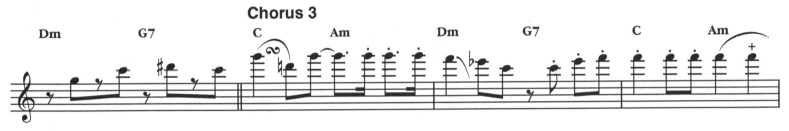

Chorus 3

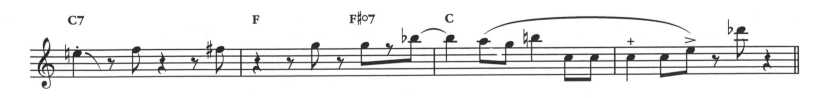

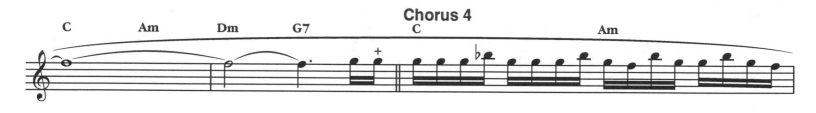

Chorus 4

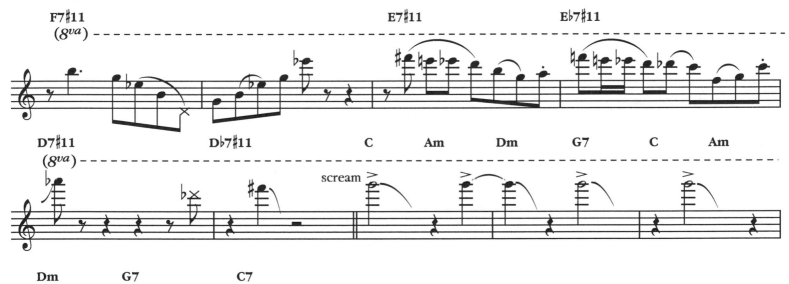

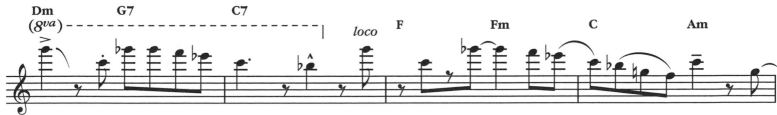

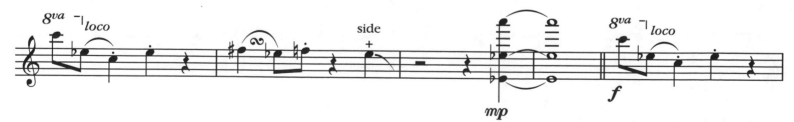

OUT OF NOWHERE

from the Paramount Picture DUDE RANCH

Soprano Sax

Words by EDWARD HEYMAN
Music by JOHNNY GREEN

Chorus 1

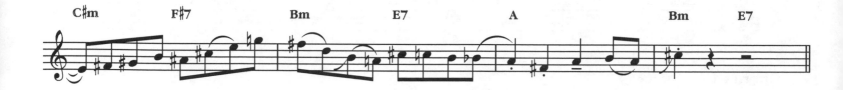

Chorus 2

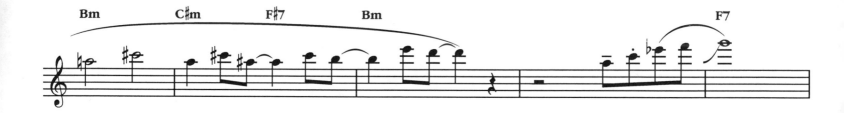

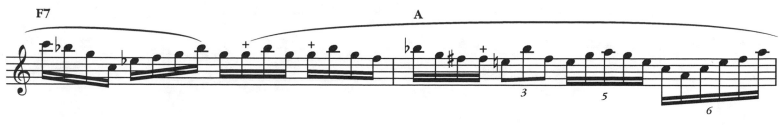

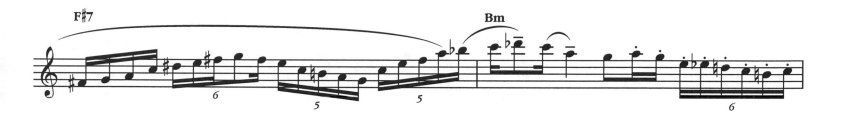

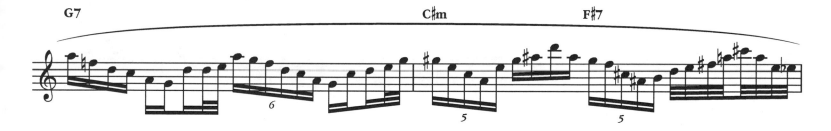

Chorus 3

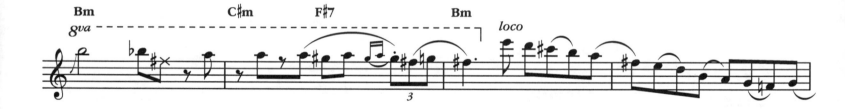

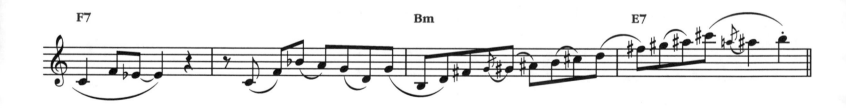

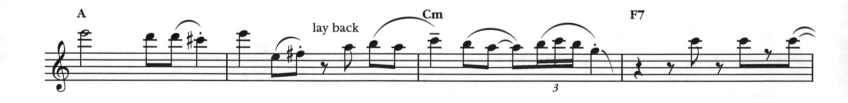

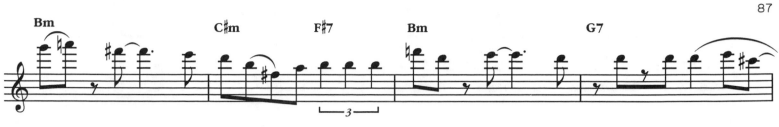

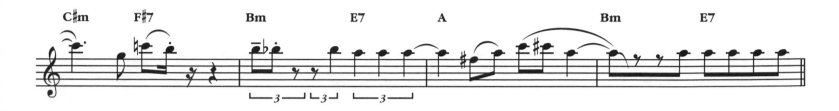

Chorus 4

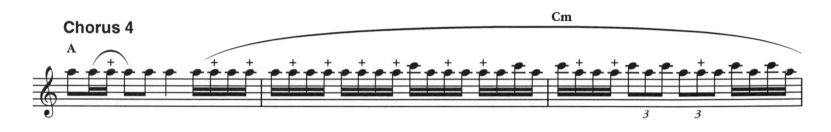

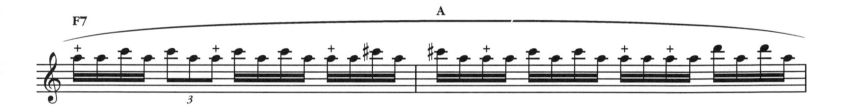

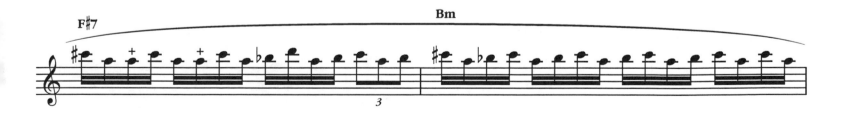

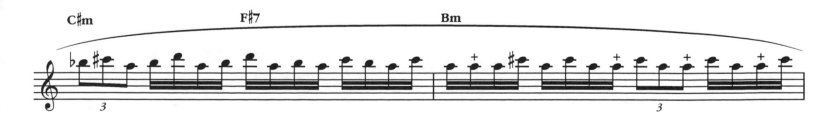

88

Chorus 5

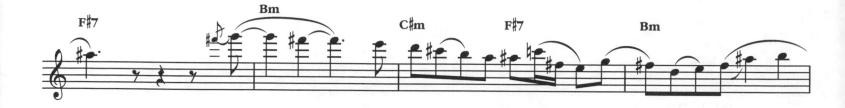

Chorus 6
delicate

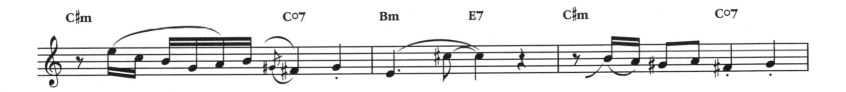

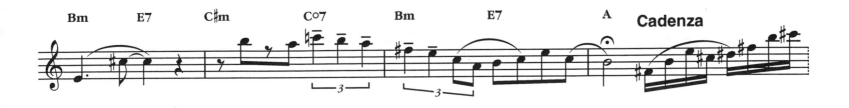

PARKER'S MOOD

Alto Sax

By CHARLIE PARKER

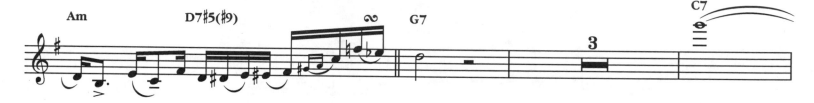

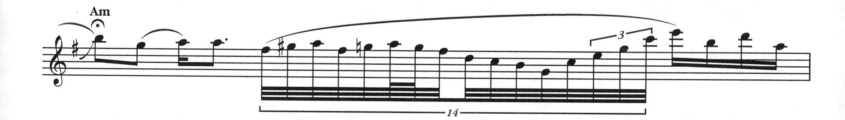